KID GUARDIANS®

JUST BE HEALTHY™ SERIES

My Trip to the Dentist

by
Diane H. Pappas, Dr. Meir Shamy
& Richard D. Covey

Illustrated by
Ric Estrada

SCHOLASTIC INC.
New York Toronto London Auckland Sydney
Mexico City New Delhi Hong Kong Buenos Aires

To my parents, Esther and Izhak, with love, the best parents ever.
And to my sister Yaffa, for her love and support, and my niece Sara, the love of my life.
—M.S.

With love to Brynne and Carson.
—R.D.C. & D.H P.

To my wife, Loretta, and our children, Aaron, Marc, Aleli, Rebekah, Seth, Jeremy, Ethan, Hannah,
and, of course, Zilia, and their spouses and children with love.
—R.E.

Thanks to the artists of The Pixel Factory (special thanks to Desma & Bob) for contributing
their talents to the creative production of these books.

ISBN-13: 978-0-545-01425-0
ISBN-10: 0-545-01425-5

12 11 10 9 8 7 6 5 4 3 2 1   7 8 9 10 11 12/0

Printed in the U.S.A.
First printing, October 2007

MEET THE KID GUARDIANS

From their home base in the mystical Himalayan mountain kingdom of Shambala, Zak the Yak and the Kid Guardians are always on alert, ready to protect the children of the world from danger.

 ZAK THE YAK is a gentle giant with a heart of gold. He's the leader of the Kid Guardians.

 Loyal and lovable, **SCRUBBER** is Zak's best friend and sidekick.

 BUZZER is both street-smart and book-smart, with a real soft spot for kids.

 Always curious about the world, **SMOOCH** loves to meet new people and see new places.

 CARROT, with her wild red hair, is funny, lovable, and the first to jump in when help is needed.

 Whenever a child is in danger, the **TROUBLE BUBBLE**™ sounds an alarm and then instantly transports the Kid Guardians to that location.

"Hurry, Mikey, or we'll be late for your dentist appointment," said Mikey's mom. "It's been six months since your last checkup "But Mom, I don't want to go!" cried Mikey.

Zak!" exclaimed Buzzer. "Mikey and his mom need our help!"
"OK, Buzzer, let's go!" Zak replied.

"Hi, I'm Zak and this is Buzzer. We help children stay safe and healthy. What's the problem, Mikey?" asked Zak.
"I'm afraid to go to the dentist," Mikey replied.

The dentist is very important," explained Zak. "The bacteria in
our mouth mixes with the food on your teeth and makes plaque."
Plaque? What's that?" asked Mikey.

Zak used his Z-Pad to show a large mouth.
"Plaque is the stuff that forms on your teeth," explained Zak.
"If plaque builds up it can cause cavities."

"Yuck," said Mikey. "How do you get rid of it?"
"Let's go to Dr. Fogleman's and find out," answered Buzzer.

"You floss plaque away by rubbing the flossing string up and down between your teeth," explained Dr. Fogleman. "You should also brush with a soft toothbrush after every meal."

f you can't brush at school, then rinse your mouth with water,"
e continued. "And remember to brush your tongue!"
My tongue, too? Wow!" said Mikey.

"If you don't keep your teeth clean, you'll get cavities and toothaches," said Zak. "And eating healthy foods will help keep your teeth strong."

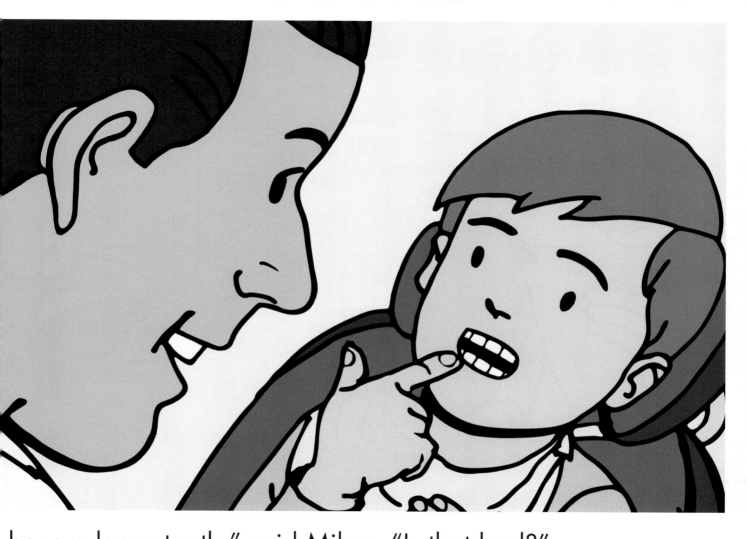

"have a loose tooth," said Mikey. "Is that bad?"

"That's normal," answered Dr. Fogleman.

"Your baby tooth is being pushed out by your permanent tooth."

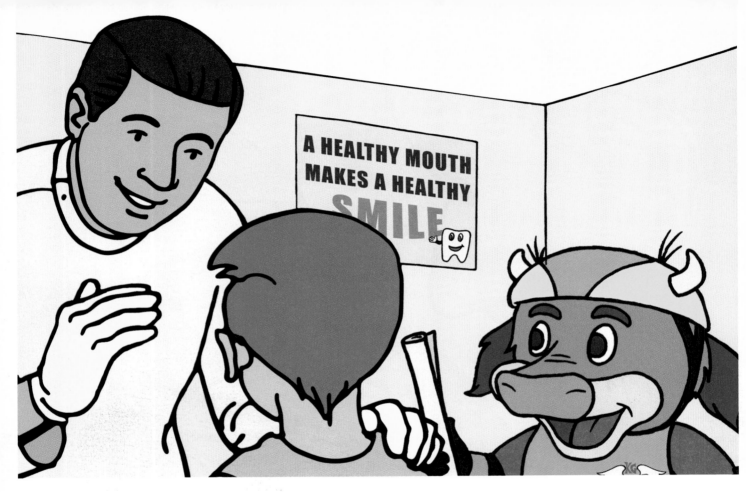

"Congratulations, a healthy mouth and no cavities," said the dentist.

"Here is a poster you can share with your class," added Buzze

"That's great!" exclaimed Mikey. "Thanks!"

"I was afraid to go to the dentist, but not anymore," said Mikey.
"He showed me how important it is to take care of my teeth.
And, to keep our teeth strong, we must eat healthy foods."

Let's remember what we learned about taking care of our teeth:

1. Floss in between your teeth after each meal.
2. Brush your teeth and tongue with a soft toothbrush after each meal.
3. If you can't brush, then rinse your mouth with water after eating.
4. Plaque forms on your teeth when bacteria in your mouth mixes with food on your teeth.